COMMUNION PRAYERS
for Holy Days *and* Holidays

This collection of communion prayers
I dedicate to Alice, my wife.
Her suggestion, followed by encouragement
and proofreading, brought to life thoughts
typed on a handful of three-by-five cards.
I owe her much more than gratitude!

COMMUNION PRAYERS
for Holy Days *and* Holidays

Alec J. Langford

CHALICE
PRESS

ST. LOUIS, MISSOURI

Cover image: W. P. Wittman Limited
Cover and interior design: Elizabeth Wright

Visit Chalice Press on the World Wide Web at
www.chalicepress.com

10 9 8 7 6 5 4 3 2 1   07 08 09 10 11 12

Library of Congress Cataloging–in–Publication Data

(pending)

Printed in the United States of America

Contents

Introduction

Skip this if you are in a hurry. You can always come back to it later.

Holy communion, the Lord's supper, the eucharist, the sacrament, ordinance, the memorial meal, the breaking of bread (I have never heard it referred to as "the drinking of wine!") or whatever the chosen title; this is the repeated sacrament of the Christian church. It remains paramount in the worship service. Celebrate it daily, weekly, monthly, quarterly, or occasionally; it still dominates the worship experience of Christians.

While I was participating as a college student in the Student Christian Movement, others whose tradition involved infrequent celebration challenged our weekly observance, hinting that familiarity breeds contempt. They did not convince me. Repeating the same rite deprives it of none of its importance. It does require deliberate attention to detail with focus on each aspect to avoid degeneration into the trivial. Whenever, however, and wherever you worship at the table, aim for this holy tradition to remain a living, vital experience for yourself and for each Christian participating.

Each generation has its particular emphases and deserves encouragement to develop unique resources. Idiom that is no longer familiar, sexist language, stilted or obscure expressions of past decades all require change, which, without undue folksiness, has been the aim in creating these prayers.

In no sense should these prayers be read as finally structured and unalterable. They are available for seeding ideas, for a change of emphasis, and for starters. Modify, adapt, and improve them for your own use. Most of all, make them truly your own prayers to your God.

The beginning of this collection of prayers came from requests by elders wanting help in finding appropriate material to use at the Lord's table. Sometimes books of communion prayers waited right before them in the church library; but in their haste, they overlooked titles that had meaning but failed to catch the attention of a harried elder. They wanted "Communion Prayers," and they wanted them ASAP with nothing else intruding.

Other volumes included so much additional material for preparation of worship services of all descriptions that searchers gave up before finding the hidden gems. Another group of books focused on polemics and hid a few examples in the back of the books. When searching for a communion prayer five minutes before the worship service starts (assuming this crisis came because of a last-minute request to be a substitute rather than from procrastination), a systematic treatise of theology misses the current objective.

In other words, I approach this pragmatically. That is why this collection freely fits the liturgical year. Here and there, additions are included based on the calendar of special days and observances.

A fresh supply of communion prayers for elders, ministers, youth leaders, retreat leaders, and group leaders—in fact, all who conduct the Lord's supper and participate as leaders— seems appropriate. We present this group of prayers for the enrichment of your worship and to the glory of God.

What guidelines lie behind these prayers, you may ask?

1. These one-purpose prayers of thanksgiving and blessing the bread and wine for the Lord's supper are usually brief.

2. As prayers, they address God, but do not pretend to inform God on the weather, the latest civic crisis, or the latest fashions. They are not pastoral prayers, nor an attempt to supply information the minister omitted from the morning sermon.

3. Prayer in this context is structured to include (speak with and for) the gathered worshiping community. Of course, it is personal, but offered on behalf of the worshipers.

4. Belief in the paramount importance of unity among Christians explains references to the Church Universal.

We commend these prayers to you hoping they provide encouragement to explore every opportunity to keep this sacrament a dignified, refined, holy exercise of the approach of the human to the divine. Blessings!

Alec J. Langford

Advent

- Begins on the Sunday nearest November 30.

- Themes include expectation, beginnings, hope, and peace—with everything focused on the coming birth of our Savior, Jesus Christ.

Advent

O God:

As we receive this ceremonial loaf, (*and/or contents of this sacramental cup*)

may our apathy be transformed to passion,

our coarse mixture of pettiness, pride, and sin be refined to purity,

our doubts absorbed into a flame of faith,

our irritability remade into graciousness, and

our distractibility into attentive wisdom.

Be born in us anew, as we thank you for this life-sustaining bread (*and/or as we receive this wine of salvation*).

We pray in the name of Jesus Christ.

Amen.

Advent

Come Emmanuel. Encourage us as we clutch our communion cups in our hands, trying to understand fully the wonderful message of Advent.

We put, side by side, hope and Advent, joy and Christmas, apprehension and Holy Week along with renewal at Easter, wondering how they come together. As we drain the cups in our hands, we have an answer in the gift and sacrifice the wine represents.

We give thanks for this sacrament of love

And, while confessing our lack of merit, are grateful for your provision of it.

In Jesus' name, we pray. Amen.

Advent

Hear our prayer, O God, as we draw near to give you
thanks for this bread (*and/or cup*).
Be merciful to us as we confess our
unworthiness to expect your forgiveness.
Inform us as we admit our indifference
to and ignorance of your wonderful ways.
Counsel us as we bring our confusion, our out-of-
place feelings, and our unwillingness to make
appropriate decisions.
Bring us peace with modulation and harmony to
replace our craziness, contentiousness, and
conflict.
Rejoice with us as we express our joy in this Advent
season.
As we accept this sacrament of your divine
intervention, we meditate again on your
compassion. Hear our prayer, O God, as we entreat
you in Jesus' name. Amen.

Hope

We are filled with hope each time we remember
the coming of the infant Jesus. Bless us in our endeav-
ors to make this world a fit place for him to dwell.

With thanksgiving, we accept these tokens of his
sacrifice for us. Make this bread and wine accentuate
our expectation of the greatest blessings we can
receive.

May the prospect of Jesus' birth enrich our whole
lives and those whom we love. We pray to you, O God,
rejoicing in your goodness and love. Amen.

Peace

Nourish us with this bread and wine, O God, to speak for peace, to witness to your love, and to work for justice. Throughout these days of Advent, bring us closer in thought to your gift of grace and goodness.

We give thanks for the Christ who was born as the expression of your generosity and caring. In these days when the temptation is upon us to be greedy, keep us from thinking that Christ was born for us alone, or that our needs transcend those of all others.

Today, as always, in our communion we remember that the one we worship went from cradle to cross, from comforted infant to crucified Christ. May our moments of thanksgiving and confession about this table humble us, renew us, bring peace and inspire us.

We pray in Christ's name. Amen.

Peace

Gracious God,

> Grant us peace.

Generate in us a longing for peace—a will to work for
> peace.

Turn us from pettiness, jealousy, and hatred.

> Open our minds and hearts to joy and hope.
> Let fear fly away.
> Let suspicion disappear.
> Let us lay aside anger and revenge.

In this Advent season of goodwill, we welcome the
> Christ child's birth with carols and chimes, as well
> as greetings from family and friends. Most of all,
> as we as ask you to bless this bread and wine, we
> thank you for Christ's sacrifice for us. We pray in
> his name and spirit. Amen.

Love

  Ever-living God, we come to you with thanksgiving
for your
  Love so amazing,
  Love so undeserved,
  Love, limitless love.
  Most vividly, we see your love in Christ's birth,
a gift that keeps changing our ways of thinking, that
continues to revolutionize the world.
  At this hour as we commune together, we pray for
your seal of approval on these elements, this bread
and wine. Bless them as we use them and re-engross
ourselves in the death and resurrection of your child,
the Christ.
  We remain ever grateful for your redeeming love
given to us. Amen.

Christmas Eve

We call Christmas glitter or enchantment, magical
  or mystical. God, as we come before you, we are
  humbled and awed.
Look over our shoulders as we complete our
  Christmas gift list. Your son remains first choice.
Throughout this service, we reverence him as we flash
  back to his birth. Fill us with hope. Irradiate us
  with your joy. Bring us to your peace.
Now, in sincerity we give thanks for each of the
  sacramental elements prepared. Bless the bread
  and wine with the richness of your saving power.
  We pray in the name of the one whose sacrifice
  made this possible, Jesus our Christ. Amen.

Christmastide

- Begins on Christmas Day and continues until the twelfth day after Christmas.

- Themes include birth and infancy of Jesus, rejoicing, hope for the future.

- Sub-themes include New Year's Eve, New Year's Day.

Christmas

Throughout this Christmas celebration, O God, we
arrange our priorities.

> Generosity not greed,
> Calm rather than chaos,
> Sharing over hoarding,
> Involvement better than withdrawal,
> Peace above conflict.

Now we look afresh at your gift to the world—
the Christ—

> Helpless babe inviting our excited greeting,
> Promised Messiah cause for ceaseless
> rejoicing.

Now at this table of remembrance, we give thanks
and ask your blessing on bread and wine. We eat
and drink in humility, giving tribute to Christ.
Amen.

Christmas

Giver of wheat and wine, God of the soil, sun, and
seed, we thank you for this sacramental cup.Founder
of faith and providence, judgment and grace, hope and
the infinite, love and limitations, we rejoice among
those who belong to the fellowship of your son Jesus
Christ.

As we journey toward Epiphany, may we focus
on those things that are of paramount importance,
putting aside lesser goals and frivolous resolutions.
We pray in the name of the one whose life gave us this
direction, whose witness gave us this sacrament, even
Jesus Christ. Amen.

Christmas

Christ's birth changed the lives of countless generations, and we acknowledge before you, God, changes he continues to make in our lives. We reveled in the good news of his coming and now face the future. As he in his life changed from helpless infant to inquisitive, questioning child, and from youth to maturity, so may we follow his example and mature as you would lead us. We go on a quest, tracing the many ways we can follow him throughout the changes and opportunities of life.

Around this table, in these moments of reflection, we come again for your blessing, both on ourselves and on this bread and wine as we live again the scenes of his sacrifice, death, and resurrection. Remain with us in our moments of need. Keep stirring us from our lapses into complacency, and refresh us in our quest of your divine service. Amen.

New Year

God, may our coming to this sacrament today seal all our vows, resolutions, and commitments for the year ahead. With penitence and gratitude, we take this bread (*and/or wine*), symbol(s) of our continued contract with you, sign(s) of our seriousness in worship, Sacrament of the church universal and reminder of the death of our Lord Jesus Christ.

Bless us in our small deeds of kindness and thoughtfulness, as in our bold and glorious plans.May courage spring from our contemplation of the sacrifice of Jesus Christ and bring nobility to our chosen courses and actions.

We accept this bread (*and/or drink this wine*) as from your hands, as your personal gift to us: through Jesus Christ our Lord. Amen.

Epiphany

- Begins January 6 and continues until Ash Wednesday—Lent.

- Themes include the visit of the magi and the baptism of Jesus.

- Sub-themes include winter, Christian unity, compassion, and race relations.

Baptism of Our Lord

Just as the Holy Spirit appeared at the baptism of our Lord, so may we in this holy communion be aware of this sacred presence and power. Sovereign One, we bless your name and ask you to make special, unique, and exceptional this bread and wine.We accept them as indications of the body and blood of Jesus.

As your guests, we covet this opportunity to recognize as part of our redemption the work, witness, and sacrifice of our Lord Jesus Christ. On this day, we also acknowledge his humility in coming to John for baptism.

Out of his full life, we glimpse ways of dedicating ourselves to peace, service, humility, and compassion. We pray that our dedication may be a worthy attempt to imitate him. Amen.

Epiphany

God, we gather to sing your praise and to give thanks for your great love and goodness. In anticipation we come again to this supper we received from your son Jesus Christ.

Make this feast signify to us what you want it to mean. We bring the bread and wine for blessing. As we come, we focus our thoughts on Christ's body and blood given, sacrificed, shed for us at his crucifixion.

Now as we receive these treasures from you, we ask for your forgiveness for every way in which we failed to live up to our commitment as Christians. Bind us in spirit to one another for support and encouragement. We pray in the blessed name of Jesus. Amen.

Epiphany

O God, our maker and maintainer, we thank you for this bread (*and/or cup*). Unite us as we receive this spiritual sustenance, this symbol of love, of sacrifice, and of nurture.

May our witness around this table speak again of the bringing together of the sacred and the profane, the spiritual and the physical. As we find our place within the sacramental community and as we see again our roots in the secular society, we pray in Christ's name. Amen.

Epiphany

We confess our unworthiness to be here, O God, as we give you thanks and prepare to share this sacrificial bread (*and/or wine*). In this moment, we live out again the sacrament, the sacrifice, the eucharist with you, our God, with all saints, and with our fellow disciples.

With you, we join in the pain, the mental torture, and the fear as they combine with our thoughts and feelings. Make us aware of our own most threatening and dehumanizing experiences. We know that as we face this table, the crucifixion of our Lord overshadows anything that can happen to us.

While it was humanity's greatest threat to overthrow decency and goodness, the resurrection turned it into an everlasting victory for us, as it has been for each Christian since our Lord triumphed over death. We thank you for that triumph.

Bless us and unite us in spirit with all generations who love and serve you. In the name of our Lord Jesus Christ, we pray. Amen.

Epiphany

With homage, we come recognizing the wonder of Jesus Christ. We reserve our highest praise for him, as did the magi following his birth.

With gifts, we recognize his worth, presenting them eagerly. Just as the wise visitors from the east came and offered their special tokens long ago, we identify him as most deserving of our gifts and worship.

As we now share together in this sacrament, we ask your blessing, O God. Let our participation here be a sign of our allegiance—our lifetime commitment. Bless, we pray, this bread (*and/or wine*) and its (*their*) connection to his sacrifice on the cross. Amen.

Epiphany

We marvel at the varied ways in which you choose to show yourself, O God. In thanksgiving, we come praising you for the revelation you are making to us today. When we think of your subtle prompting to stir stargazers from a far country to visit the infant Jesus, we see how you reached out everywhere to introduce the Messiah.

Without reservation, we, too, hail him and bow before him in reverence. With gladness, we know he came not only to kings, conquerors, scholars, and sophisticates, but also to shepherds, fisher people, tax collectors, along with the poor and powerless.

Unite us all, rich and poor, simple and smart, powerful and powerless, to humble ourselves before you as we bless these sacramental elements and receive them for our spiritual nutrition. In Jesus' name, we pray. Amen.

Winter

God, our protector, be close to us throughout this winter season, as we cherish the closeness of Christian friends. We look forward from the bleakness of these days to the promise of brighter days ahead. Teach us patience with the seasons, in their constancy and in the variety they bring to our lives.

Whenever we worship you, we come with thanksgiving that life presents more than climate and external circumstance. Teach us to look inward, treasuring spiritual gifts. Most precious is the gift of your son Jesus. At this table, we remember his sacrificial death and ask your blessing on this bread (*and/or wine*). Enrich us spiritually throughout all our days. Amen.

Unity

We reflect, O God, on your goodness, purity, and faithfulness as we accept this sacramental cup. Bless us with its refreshing and enriching drops. May we be found worthy to receive this gift. Keep us mindful of the privilege with which it is accompanied.

Come into our presence as risen Lord. Come into our lives to remind us of your purity. Come with us as we are challenged to share with each other, to stand for truth, to witness to your loving care, and to be renewed.

We give thanks for this cup, as we thank you, God, for the one whose sacrifice brought us here, related us to one another, and keeps us united. Our prayer is in Jesus' name. Amen.

Unity

Gather us together around this table;
>Join us with you, O God, in an unbreakable unity,
>So that as we share this cup, (*these holy elements*)
>We may be fully conscious
>Of your sacrifice so costly,
>Of your love so generous.
>We pray in Jesus' name.
>Amen.

Compassion

We come, unstinting God, to this act of sharing bread and wine.
>With thankfulness, we receive your unmatched gifts.
>With confession, we admit to our lack of preparation to be in your presence.
>With joy, we gather with your people.
>Above all, we value the sacrifice and offer of salvation by your son Jesus Christ.
>In his name, we pray.
>Amen.

Compassion

We approach this sacrament, confessing our unworthiness and inadequacy, O God. As we come, we pray for your forgiveness because we need it new each day.

Thank you again for your gift of this bread (*and/or cup*) and all that it meant to you and means to us. Let that generosity and compassion not just shock and frighten us. Let them motivate and enable us. In our world of hurts, ills, punishments, and disasters, may we become part of the healing, rewarding, and blessing. Focus our giving not just on people we deem deserving, but on all your children; not just toward the grateful, but also to the rude and unmindful.

We pray in the name of the one who showed us the way, enticed us with love, compassion, and understanding, even our Lord Jesus Christ. Amen.

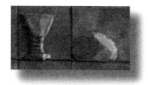

Lent

- Begins Ash Wednesday. Continues forty days to the eve of Easter.

- Themes include preparation, penitence, introspection; focus is on the concluding weeks of our Lord's ministry.

- Sub-themes include spring.

Lent ──────────────────

Ash Wednesday

With penitence, we join Christians around the
world on this first day of Lent. At your holy table, we
lift our voices in thanks for these simple elements—
the bread and wine—praying that you, our God, will
bless and sanctify them.

Assist us as we confess our shortcomings and plan
to move ahead in our lives from remorse to resolve,
from regret to renewal. We pray for Christ's presence
with us as we journey toward Easter with the triumph
of the resurrection.

Tune our minds to the holy, to your overarching
goodness and love. Keep our steps firmly planted on
the path toward your truth. In Christ's name, we pray.
Amen.

Lent

As we enter anew into the Lenten season, we come
around your table, O God, awakened to our spiritual
deficiencies, conscious of our opportunities, and
aware of your resources. Bring us together as we break
bread and drink from the cup.

Open our eyes to opportunities for service and
sacrifice. Keep us true to the genius of your church's
witness. Keep us loyal to your church's ecumenical
vision, and keep us burning with your church's
evangelical zeal. May we be sincere imitators of your
son's self-giving, kindness, and love. We pray in his
name. Amen.

Lent

We relent, we disown, and we relinquish all that could keep us from communion with you, merciful God. Hear our thanksgiving as we blend it with confession while we receive this bread (*and/or cup*) and unite ourselves with you and your children everywhere.

We give thanks, as well, for the message of hope and assurance given by your son, and for his saving act in which we share as we worship together.

In Jesus' name, we pray. Amen.

Lent

God, we worship around this table that your son prepared with his disciples. Having been given a place at the table, may we be grateful to receive this bread of remembrance (*and/or cup of blessing*) and sacrifice, and may we graciously share with any who need your love.

Broaden our compassion, build on our understanding, and strengthen our devotion as we receive this sacrament in the season of Lent. May these intimate moments identify us anew with your great plan for humanity and your caring for every one of us. We confess our less than nominal performance as Christians, and we give thanks for your gift to us.

In Jesus' name, we pray. Amen.

Lent

O God, we give thanks for this sacrament of everlasting love.May our full human stature be realized as we partake of the bread—symbol of the total sacrifice of Jesus Christ, your son. We confess our human failures and unworthiness to share Christ's complete love and unswerving devotion. Accept our contrition, and enhance our resolve to be true to you.

Fill us with joy in sharing with those surrounding us and with all Christians who accept your life-giving feast this day. Unite us in understanding and sympathy with those who cannot commune with us today.

In Jesus' name, we pray. Amen.

Lent

God, we know you never make fools of us, but we often make fools of ourselves. We confess our foolery, foolishness, and our downright foolhardiness.

Today as we make communion, we know there is no connection with anything foolish in either its concept or its completion. (There we go again making foolishness of something foolproof.) If ever we are tempted to take lightly these elements of communion representing the body and lifeblood of our Lord, let it not be here. Let it not in any way be connected with the superb manner in which this was done for the least of us, the best of us, and for all who take your name.

Cheer us once more as we come to this sublime moment, as we dedicate and rededicate ourselves to this new day for your church. Amen.

Lent

We behold your self-sacrifice, O God, as we accept this bread (*and/or cup*) today. We hold this beside our memories and perception of all other human sacrifices. Keep us clear in our definitions either of noble sacrifice or of irrational and deceptive abandon.

Hear our confession of complicity in the offense and scandal of events such as those that led to the passion of our Lord, and purify us as we bring this bread (*and/or cup*) to our lips. We pray for forgiveness from you as we trust you, loving God, to enlighten us in the ways of your shalom. In Jesus' name, we pray. Amen.

Lent

Lord, for this life-changing experience at your table, we give thanks. Bless the bread before us. As we break it, we pray for deepened insight into the blessing that the sacrament confers on us.

Hear our confession as we measure ourselves by the divine standards you demonstrated through your son, Jesus.

May we in this Lenten season renew our vows, strengthen our resolve to serve justice and peace, oppose all degradation of the human spirit, and constantly seek your divine guidance.

As we meditate on Jesus' challenges for us to turn the other cheek, to become keepers of the less fortunate, go deeper into compassion, to serve rather than command, we seek strength.

In his name, we pray. Amen.

Lent

God, we ask for your blessing upon this sacred meal we have come to share with Christians here and everywhere. We come with confessions. Because we know of your grace and mercy, we ask for forgiveness.

Before we partake of this bread (*and/or wine*), we thank you not only for it (*or them*) but for Christ's sacrifice, which brings hope to our lives. May his giving to the end fill us with determination to make more of every day of our lives. For his sake, we pray. Amen.

Compassion

For this nourishing element, we give thanks to you, O God. Just as food and drink sustain our bodies, may our spirits be refreshed, strengthened, and renewed through the love expressed in this sacrament.

As we recall the meaning of the broken body (*and/or shed blood*) in terms of human sacrifice, of pain, even of life itself, we stop in our casual, careless drift from one thought to another, from one deed to another. We confess all our willfulness and waste, our making the holy trivial, and our trumping up trivia to godly proportions. In your goodness, O God, we entreat you to forgive us.

We pray in Christ's name. Amen.

Spring

Along with the blessings you have showered upon us, O God, we give thanks for the glories of springtime. As we revel in this season of promise, growth, change, transformation, and hope, we give you praise.

Around this table as we worship, we again think of promise, growth, change, transformation, and hope— all these things you have given us in Jesus Christ.

Accept our request that this bread and wine receive your blessing. As we take them for our spiritual nourishment, may our praise continue.

In the name of our Lord, we pray. Amen.

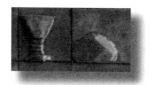

Holy Week

- Begins on Palm Sunday and continues to Easter Sunday.

- Themes include triumphal entry, celebration, the Lord's supper, betrayal, arrest, trial, crucifixion.

Holy Week

We have gathered as your guests, O God.

May we be worthy to receive the wealth of your gifts for us. We give thanks for this bread (*and/or cup*), thanks that come from our deep gratitude.

Move among us as our host, we pray, while in this sacramental meal we welcome, and say farewell to friends, as we grieve and as we rejoice. Our hearts are stirred by the rich meaning that envelops this simple feast. Our minds are enticed to flash between your son's feast of love with his disciples and our sharing in this thanksgiving meal.

Rekindle in us the spirit of love and caring. Remove from us the haughtiness that tempts us to think we have a special right to this table. In Jesus' servant spirit, refresh our memories as to who we are. We ask for courage to keep from pettiness and greed, from lust and selfishness, from thoughtlessness and self-imposed ignorance. Amen.

Palm Sunday

We join in praise, O God, as did Jesus' admirers on Palm Sunday. We rejoice and celebrate along with the throngs. Words and shouts come from our lips as readily as they did from those of the pilgrims and well-wishers on the way to Jerusalem. May we see him anew—challenging, fresh, and vital.

As we gather in these moments to exult in thanksgiving around the Lord's table, we would bring into this holy place more than our excitement. We would also make this a sacrament by our vows of loyalty to our Lord.

While we take this bread (*and/or cup*) in memory of the death of our Savior, we accept with it our opportunity to serve you and to share in tasks of your kingdom. Knowing that Holy Week has dedication, anxiety, pain, and sacrifice flowing out of the pleasures of Palm Sunday, we accept our tasks anew and dedicate ourselves again to your son Jesus Christ Amen.

Palm Sunday

All-knowing God, our rejoicing this day comes from your love and concern for us. We thank you for Jesus' confidence, his sharing with friends on Palm Sunday, and for the inspiration he provides us every Sunday as we commemorate his death in this eucharist. Bless the bread (*and/or wine*) as we receive it (*or them*) and relate what we are doing to his sacrifice and his love.

May this be an act of renewal within a day of renewal and anticipation. May he ride in triumph through our city and across our land. May his message be heard throughout the world. In Jesus' name, we pray. Amen.

Palm Sunday

O God, we thank you for the courage shown by Christ throughout his triumphal entry. We marvel at his ability to rise above depression and face the crowds, knowing the other dreadful procession that stretched ahead of him. We wonder over his mastery of the situation, enabling him to ride above despair and showing he would not yield to temptation or pressure to move out of character to become a zealot or leader of a rebel mob.

As we eat this bread (*and/or drink this cup*), make us aware that some of our Calvaries come after Palm Sundays. We accept this reminder with thanks and humility in Jesus' name. Amen.

Maundy Thursday

As the first gathering in the upper room challenged loyalties, prejudices, truth, and justice, O merciful God, may we be prepared for surprises, stresses and new insights on this special evening.

We open ourselves to your divine scrutiny as we confess weakness and failure of resolve. We pray for forgiveness to be made real to us in this celebration of communion.

For the body and blood of your son Jesus, we give thanks as we take the elements of bread and wine placed before us. Bless these symbols, and renew our spiritual vigor as we continue our pilgrimage to the triumph of Easter. In Jesus' name, we pray. Amen.

Good Friday

On this day with its tragic associations, we pause before this table, O God, to give you thanks for the bread and wine. Bless and sanctify them. Bring us again to the stark reality of human sin as it looms before us in Calvary—before our Savior who sacrificed his life for us.

While we accept these elements of a life given over to death, let us keep clearly in our consciousness the vision of Easter with its resurrection hope. Renew us, we pray. Accompany us to each of our Calvaries. In Jesus' name, we ask this. Amen.

Eastertide

- Begins Easter Sunday and continues to Pentecost, seven Sundays later.

- Themes include resurrection and rejoicing.

- Sub-themes include Mother's Day, Christian Family life, Rural Life, and Memorial Sunday (depending on the date upon which Easter falls).

Easter Sunrise

Like the rising sun, hope and confidence burst upon us as we contemplate Jesus' resurrection. May we, almighty God, never lose the transformation Christ's resurrection brought both to disciples and to followers of his day, as well as to succeeding generations of Christians who, like ourselves, wait for the fullness of this truth.

Bless with the richness of your approval these fruits of the grain stalk and the vine that we now see on this plate and in this chalice. Consecrate us as we receive them, that in change and revitalization our lives may bring praise to you and encouragement to other human beings.

We give thanks for Jesus Christ, in whose courage and suffering we now live new lives. We give thanks to you for this Easter day of gladness. Amen.

Easter

On this holy and happy day of the resurrection, we give thanks, gracious God, for this bread (*and/or cup*), the symbol(s) of your dying and of your undying love for us. We gather for this confession of our needs, for this renewal of our vows, for this rejoicing over the way you have accepted us, encouraged us, and nurtured us.

Hear us in our grief, listen to us in our need, pity us in our weakness, heal us in our suffering, correct us in our arrogance, and love us in our dependence. We eat this bread (*and/or drink from this cup*), which is a sign of our acceptance of a sacred covenant. We have joined in this hour of worship as an expression of our care for one another. We have united with Christians here and everywhere to declare to the whole world that Christ lives in and through us. In his name, we pray. Amen.

Second Sunday of Easter

Drive us through familiar experiences of worship into the special place of your sanctuary, creator God. Keep us from satisfaction or boredom with the familiar. Bring us back to the holy thoughts and pure motives that surround this table and your saints who have communed here.

In our meditation on tragedy, let us take this bread (*and/or cup*) again with senses alert to your ennobling and cleansing. That you have brought redemption through senseless violence, death, and shame grounds us in our struggle to make sense of events around us. We pray in the name of Jesus Christ. Amen.

Eastertide

Grant, compassionate God, that our coming together
around this table may be to each of us a source of new
strength.

Speak to us through the sacrifice of our Lord,
through the elements of the sacrament,
through the association with each other;
That life may become
more exciting to some who found it dull,
simpler for those caught in its complexity,
happier for those who have tangled with grief,
friendlier for the isolated or ostracized,
safer for the vulnerable or defenseless,
calmer for the stressed and anxious,
and holier for those estranged from beauty or
goodness.

We give our thanks for this bread (*and/or wine*) and
ask your blessing. Amen.

Eastertide

God of all people, we give thanks for this bread (*and/or cup*)—essence, symbol, and guarantee of your love for us. May these moments represent more than thanksgiving, contrition, introspection, confession, and amendment.

With all your friends and loved ones around the world, we rejoice in common values, strength, love, and the infusion of Jesus' spirit. Unite us in a world that mixes greed and selfishness, distrust and anger in volatile concoctions—not to be subverted by it, but to bring hope, challenge, and love to those in need. In Jesus' name, we pray. Amen.

Eastertide

Creator God, our life source, as we contemplate these days marking the beginning Church's first great expansion, may we, too, be ready and eager for changes and surprises in the life of today's Church. We thank you for the fresh hope we gathered as we celebrated Easter and now look forward to Pentecost.

In each of our celebrations of this holy meal, awaken us to visions of your truth—truth that can enhance and change our lives. If it includes changes of direction, we expect to heed them and prosper through them.

Now in thankfulness we pray for your blessings on this bread and wine. Through Christ's death and resurrection, we know its vital quality. Amen.

Eastertide

In the name of the one, Jesus the Christ, we pray to you, our God. Bring us this day to the awareness we need to celebrate fully this holy sacrament. We join now with all Christians who, whether free or fettered, remember his death as they break bread and drink wine together. In our worship may we also appreciate the "great cloud of witnesses" whose presence enriches us and will continue to inspire us.

Bless this bread and this cup. In our thankfulness may we overlook their ordinariness, not taking them for granted but understanding them in their sacramental power. Amen.

Rural Life

Our spirits, O sustaining God, are lifted when we see your glory in the world stretched out before us. We find your touch in nature and the wonders of your creatures small and great.

Refocus our attention to connect with not only your superbly crafted creation, but also with your feeling for and understanding of all conditions of the human spirit. We place our weakness and frailty beside your strength and eternity.

In this communion, we give thanks for the bread and wine, knowing you have shared with us in a world-shaking event. We memorialize the Christ who made this gift possible and who continues with us. Amen.

Earth Day

God, Creator of us all, our reverence for your design prompts us to come to this, your table, confessing failure to act or to speak decisively showing our respect, our understanding, and resolve to cherish and improve. When we take bread and wine—simple, basic, yet precious products of the earth—we come to this communion alerted to our responsibility.

God, our Savior, accept us still as we remember in your presence Christ's death for our sakes. Knowing our status as guests at this celebration, we give you deference, gratitude, and devotion. Be our guide as we, throughout our days on this earth, endeavor to live as good stewards. Again, we covet your blessing. Amen.

Mother's Day

God, on this day when we remember tenderness and devotion, caring and nurturing, comfort and support, giving and sacrifice, we turn again to you. With thanks, we remember Christ and his sacrifice on our behalf.

Heighten our understanding of what Calvary meant for him and means today for us. We take this cup and savor its drops of divine love.

Strengthen our renewed resolve to be caring and nurturing. We choose to walk in the steps of the master and to face the demands made upon us as well as the joys he shared with us.

Broaden our love and understanding as we rely on you to parent and protect us. We pray for your guidance, your direction, and your vision. In Jesus' name, we pray. Amen.

Family

Today, O God, be near to us as we confront this sacred place, this table, these elements, and the wealth of memories brought before us. Remind us of communion past, the joy of family and friends who have joined with us in this celebration.

We give thanks to you, our God, for Jesus, his life, his truth, his sacrifice, and his salvation. We pray that we may be worthy to receive your spirit.

Bless to each one of us the bread and wine offered in memory of your saving love, and care for us.

Consecrate us, we pray in Jesus' name. Amen.

Memorial Weekend

In memory of the Savior's love, O God, we assemble at this table, giving thanks for these elements. Bless for our spiritual use this bread and wine. While we remember in this season all who have given their lives for honor, integrity, and truth, we are always elevating this sacrament, praying for more faithfulness, deeper devotion, and the bonding that keeps us strong in our beliefs.

We confess again our insignificance, our worthlessness, and untrustworthy past. Keep us truthful as we confess our own faults and not those of our neighbors. We pray in Jesus' name. Amen.

Pre-Pentecost

Eternal God, we have brought before you our sacrifice of praise and thanksgiving. We freely offer our gifts of love and service. O God, in gratitude we join our minds at this table with its spiritual menu. For this cup of generous, free, and willing sacrifice we thank you. For Jesus Christ whose blood it represents, we thank you.

In so doing we join the generations of faithful witnesses who brought us the good news of his life, death, and resurrection.In the bonds of faith and through the strength of your Holy Spirit may we continue both as conscientious disciples in your kingdom now and as it continues to come in all its fullness. We pray in Jesus name. Amen.

42

Pre-Pentecost

Lord, we come with thanksgiving for your generosity to us, accepting us in our temerity beside your greatness. Expand our gratitude.

Lord, we come with confession, facing up to our errors while fully aware of your holiness. Develop our humility.

Lord, we come with our ignorance, yet knowing your wisdom. Deepen our confidence.

Lord, we come fainthearted, without understanding or courage. Build our strength.

Bless now the bread we break (*and/or the wine we drink*), the symbolic body (*and/or blood*) of your son. Accept each one of us, fill us, and use us. In Jesus' name, we implore you. Amen.

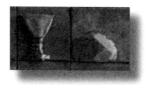

Pentecost

- Begins the seventh Sunday after Easter.

- Themes include the gift of the Holy Spirit, the Trinity, and the ministry of Christ.

- Sub-themes include freedom, democracy, summer, Labor Day, world communion, ministry, All Saints' Day, reformation, thanksgiving, reconciliation.

Pentecost

Draw us by your spirit, O God, out from beyond our narrow concerns and selfish desires, way out from whatever would allow us to enthrone ourselves and push you aside.

Draw our thoughts together at this table in this opportunity to share, sympathize, trust, and triumph as we join our Lord.

We express thanks for this cup into which meaning has been poured, where the essence and vitality of Jesus' life is found. As we move beyond our memories and reminiscences, bless us, we pray, in the name of our Lord Jesus Christ. Amen.

Pentecost

Ever-refreshing Spirit, be with us as we celebrate and seek renewal in this sacrament.

Spirit that purifies, Spirit that clears away dross, Spirit that comes as a surprise with power and enlightenment, be present as we take this bread (*and/ or cup*).Renew us in our passion for the unity of all of your people, O God.

Bless this sacred bread (*and/or cup*) for which we give our thanks. May our lives, through its nourishment, come closer to your love and perfection. In Jesus' name, we pray. Amen.

Trinity Sunday

Have mercy upon us, O God. Have mercy as we gather around this table. We mingle our confession and our thanksgiving as we contemplate your spirit moving among us. We give thanks for the bread (*and/or cup*), with the emblem(s) that it (*or they*) represent(s).

We reach out to each other with pleas for grace and forgiveness. Be with us in our communing, as you have always been in our moments of closeness and devotion, as well as in times of our indifference and defiance. In Jesus' name. Amen.

Pentecost

In your infinite wisdom, O God, you have communicated with us through these elements of bread and wine that supply our need for nourishment. Ferment in us, as yeast ferments in dough, your most holy desires and designs.

Just as fresh bread excites our palate, bring us around this table for fresh, vital ideas, for inspiration, for hope. Symbolically, we have joined in this meal, expecting to be energized for the tasks of the Church. Keep ever before us the Christ, who brought us together by his example, inspiration, and sacrifice. We pray in his name. Amen.

Pentecost

We thank you, O God, for this bread and wine we receive from your hand. We thank you for your son, Christ, whose body and blood bring to us perspective and symbol, sacrifice and mysterious love. Bless, we pray you, each one who has come to share in this thanksgiving meal, to rejoice in your presence with us, to affirm again the spirit and reality of your Church, and to live again for you.

Unite us in ties of reconciliation, of compassion, and of gratitude. Confessing our failures, omissions, carelessness, and self-deluding lies, we come in humility to this, your table. In Jesus' name, we pray. Amen.

Pentecost

As these plain items, the bread and wine, are placed before us, merciful God, we ask your blessing on them and on each of those who share them today. With gratitude, we recognize their blessed meaning—making real today the body and blood of Jesus—linking us to the atonement offered through his sacrifice.

We recall that he walked among his people, shared his truth about you, showed his compassion for those in need, and freely healed the sick. While we abhor the terrible death he suffered, we rejoice in everything he brought us through both his life and his death on our behalf. In his name, we offer this prayer. Amen.

Pentecost

As we gather again for this sacrament, almighty God, we suspect we have brought with us hidden baggage. From our human stress, anxiety, depression, repose, abandon, or elation, may we each become aware of our potential for change and improvement.

Now, as we hold before you the bread to be broken (*and/or the cup to be poured*), we pray that you will bless and sanctify it (*or them*). May its (*or their*) reality, representing the body (*and/or blood*) of Christ, transform us.

Send us again to the world as we contemplate this newness of life. Use us as your agents of change, enlightenment, benevolence, and most of all of your love. Our prayer is in Christ's name, whose example sets us on a path to perfection. Amen.

Pentecost

We pray to you, our God, in thankfulness. Bless this bread and wine, we ask, in Jesus' name.

When we join around this table, our minds are tested as we open up in thought this high point in his ministry. We seat ourselves in that room where this epic event unfolds.

Enable the holiness of this occasion to erase petty struggles for preference in the kingdom. Use the uniqueness of this place to erase consideration of betrayal that marred the celebration of the Twelve. Strengthen again our determination to stay focused on lofty and pure goals as we receive the elements of this sacrament. Amen.

Pentecost

In this sacred hour, O merciful God, we come ready to receive your divine gifts at this altar. Bless these tokens—bread and wine—we have brought. Impart the measure of Christ's sacrifice of his body and blood that we can bear as we meditate upon this transformation, this making of the mundane into the sacred.

Our thanks we pour out to you as we attempt to attire ourselves with compassion, kindness, humility, meekness, and patience. In these brief moments, we would re-equip ourselves for our life of witness to your truth, your salvation.

In this sacred hour, we yield ourselves to Christ's way. Keep us true to his unquestioning obedience, his life given in sacrificial love. Amen.

Pentecost

May our delight be in your law, O Lord. We come from our world of cares and pleasures, hoping in this time of self-searching and communing with you to fix our priorities and to rise to new heights of dedication for your sake and for your kingdom.

On these plates and in these cups we see familiar bread and fruit of the vine. We bring them to this table with thanksgiving and pray for your blessing. Transform them, and convert each of us to serve your purposes, to experience and live in your grace and love.

We focus again on our Christ, through whom this change and renewal comes. Let us never leave without grasping a fresh vision of the magnificence of his sacrifice for us. Amen.

Freedom and Democracy

Set us free with your truth, O God. Release us in spirit that we may grant to others what we find in you. Free our minds from the shortcuts into new tyranny—of violence, of selfishness, of disregard for others' rights, others' beliefs, or cherished hopes.

In this bread (*and/or cup*) that we bless, may we find the challenge and renewal that you freely offered to us. We give you thanks for the truth, which it (*or they*) represent(s), for the vision of sacrifice and redemption that it (*or they*) contain(s).

Seal our lives with the covenant that this sacrament guarantees. We pray in the name of our Lord Jesus Christ, in whose bondage is our real freedom.

Amen.

Freedom and Democracy

God, instiller of goodness and mercy in human beings, we brought you our gifts throughout this worship in prayer, in music, in hymns, in homily, meditation, and offering.

We now come to share in the depth of this sacrament, your sacrifice that communicates to us your intense abhorrence of sin, the breadth of your love, and the height of your compassion.

Lord, we seek a broadening of our grasp on the meaning of freedom: freedom to be willful, freedom to be understanding, freedom to live and let live.

Accept our thanks for this bread and cup. May they nurture and tincture our whole view of life and each other. Through Jesus' name, we pray. Amen.

Summer

Hear our prayer, creator God, as we thank you for the sunshine, warmth, brightness, change, and growth of this season. While we bow in awe at the variety and multiplicity of your works in the world around us, we admire the works of your spirit among us.

In your spirit of holiness, we seek to grow, to diversify, and to produce; but for renewal, we come to this table. We cherish the sacramental gifts that come from grain and grapes and have placed them here with thankfulness. Bless this bread and wine as we partake with gratitude. Stand beside us as we humbly serve you. In Jesus' name, we pray. Amen.

Pentecost

We take this blessed bread (*and/or this sacred cup*), O God, and share in the sacrament that unites us to you and to our Christian sisters and brothers everywhere. As we share in these moments of reflection, it is with gratitude we stand before you. O God, it is with humility we admit to our need for your forgiveness and love.

Strengthen us to join in common cause for your truth and justice, as we long for the coming of your kingdom in its fullness and glory. As we eat this bread (*and/or drink this wine*), it is with our pledge and dedication. May it entice us forward to the extension of your righteousness both in our lives and with people everywhere. We pray in the name of our Lord Jesus Christ. Amen.

Pentecost

O God, we come to this table to express our common needs, our common strengths. As we take this bread (*and/or this cup*); we reach out to you who in love, forgiveness, and divine compassion met us with your son Christ.

We come to this table to commune and to reach spiritual depths. We come to remove barriers in our self-understanding. We come also to remove barriers between ourselves and you, as well as obstacles we have created between others and ourselves. We thank you for all who share this planet with us. We take this holy bread (*and/or sacred cup*), O God, and share in the sacrament that unites us to you and to our Christian sisters and brothers everywhere.

Our confession and our thanks go to the one whose life and whose pain made this possible, even Jesus Christ our Lord. Amen.

Pentecost

This bread and wine, O God, symbolically speak volumes to us in our affluence, telling us to share as Christ shared. In our need and poverty, this bread and wine motion us toward our Lord, who was "despised and rejected."

The eucharist we share freely challenges us to tear down barriers of racism, sexism, and classism. This sacrament challenges us to partake of one food and be made one. Where illness and death stalk us, this sacrament provides a window through which we glimpse your divine love, our hope. We give thanks for Christ Jesus. We give thanks for these moments of remembering the act that takes us back to Calvary and sends us forward, confident of your abiding presence. Amen.

Pentecost

Red wine! We have in this cup, blushing and flushed, red wine. It has flowed and fermented, refined and matured. We sip from it and give thanks. Who wants a sacrament made out of weak tea or stale coffee? Who wants a sacrament built on sudden impulse to be noble and great?

O God, this feast we celebrate compels us to bow in contrition, to give you thanks and ask your blessing. We witness such strong feelings, feelings that grow from the willing, purposeful, generous sacrifice made for us by Jesus Christ. Amen.

Pentecost

Today, O God, we draw the present together with time long past. We confess our unworthiness to be here, as, in the next breath, we give thanks. We share this sacrificial bread (*and/or wine*). In this moment—the now, the present—we live out again the sacrament, the sacrifice, the eucharist with you, our God.

With you, we join in the pain, the mental torture, and the fear of Calvary. These emotions combine with our thoughts and feelings, making us remember experiences that were to us most intimidating and dehumanizing. We know that as we face this table, the crucifixion of our Lord was history's greatest threat to overthrow decency and goodness. Yet in the resurrection, this is a moment of triumph for us, as it has been for each Christian since our Lord triumphed over death.

Bless us and unite us in spirit with all generations who love and serve you. In the name of our Lord Jesus Christ, we pray. Amen.

Pentecost

Break again your bread of life, caring God, that we may enter your marvelous kingdom.

Break again your bread of life, sustaining God, that we may be fully alive in your spirit that keeps refreshing, maintaining, and enticing us out of our hibernation of contentment.

Break again your bread of life, righteous God, that we may see vividly your goodness and truth, and shun evil and wrong.

As we give thanks for this loaf of the sacrifice, this element of the eucharist, we pray for your blessing both on this act of worship and on all who come to this feast bringing their commitment and their devotion. In Jesus' name, we pray. Amen.

Pentecost

O God,

Pour out again your truth that grapples with and grieves over our unseemly anger, hate, jealousy, and pride.

Pour out again your wine of justice that we drink, knowing full well it clashes with our exaggerated demand for revenge, our play on shame, our destructive competition, and even our feeling that we deserve all the breaks.

Pour out again your lifeblood in love that counts no cost too high, no person too worthless, no deed too vile to receive your forgiveness and salvation. We pray in the name of Jesus. Amen.

Pentecost

Whenever we are devalued, O God, you revalue us. We accept this sacred bread (*and/or cup*) as a sign, knowing it represents hope, enrichment, and the generous gift of your son.

We give thanks as we recognize that all life-giving and sustaining gifts come from you.

Keep changing us to what you want us to be. We admit our imperfection, willfulness, and stubbornness. We pray in the name of the only perfect one—our Lord Jesus Christ. Amen.

Pentecost

Lift this humble product of the field, sunshine, and baker's skill to the holy use for which we now dedicate it.

We pray, all-knowing God, that you will accept our thanks—not alone for these crumbs of bread so transitory—but for your son's sacrifice so everlasting.

Stir this fruit of the vine, ferment it, flavor it, foster in it all the goodness and forgiveness, love and lasting compassion that made it a world-changing sacrament.

Engross us in this sacrifice, this remarkable event, and make us forever yours, in Christ Jesus. Amen.

Pentecost

Remind us, O God, as we take this cup,
    of the shabby treatment given your perfect son.
Renew us, O God, as we drink this cup
    and review the vastness of your love and grace.
Receive us, O God, as we drain this cup
    and present ourselves for your forgiveness.
Recycle us, O God, as we commune,
    and give ourselves anew to the work of your
        kingdom,
    your Church, your children. In Jesus' name.Amen.

Pentecost

May your kingdom continue to come in our lives, almighty God. Enable its coming throughout the people in the world around us, we pray. Use us as your instruments of truth, peace, and justice as we seek to be of service to you.

Test us with your holiness and perfection as we approach you through these elements of the eucharist. For the bread and wine, we give you thanks as we ask you to bless them for us.

Make us aware of those around us as we appreciate the strength of your Church making its appeal to all manner of people In their poverty and wealth, in their youth and maturity, in their ignorance and their wisdom. Maintain your spirit of holiness among us all. In Jesus' name, we pray. Amen.

Pentecost

Your kingdom come throughout the Church.
Your kingdom come closer and closer to the world.
Your kingdom come, majestic God, in our minds and throughout our whole beings.

As we eat this bread (*and/or drink this cup*), make us conscious of the impediments to your realm of love. May we see vividly that sacrifice, giving, surrender, as Jesus verified, were kingdom-related acts. With fervor we choose your way. In Jesus' name, we entreat you to bless this element (*or these elements*) and each of us receiving it (*or them*). Amen.

Pentecost

O God:
Bread is baked.
Bread is broken.
Bread is blessed.
OR
Wine is ripened.
Wine is poured.
Wine is blessed.

We take it in token of love expressed,
Of sin acknowledged,
Of forgiveness extended,
Of guilt ended.

We give thanks to Christ the ever-giving,
to God the ever-living.
Amen.

Pentecost

Bless this bread and this wine, we pray, generous God. We have gathered in thanksgiving to acknowledge again your love that sacrificed all of self. We celebrate again the strength of your son who flinched not at injustice and cruelty. We acknowledge again your goodness that stooped to come among us and to live with our imperfection: our impatience, our fickleness, and our lack of insight into your great design.

Unite us once again in this simple, spiritual meal with saints who have sung your praise and served you through joy and adversity. Let us stand beside those who have recently given their allegiance to you and need sustenance and assurance. Identify us also with those whose lives are impoverished, that we all may draw closer to the one who knew poverty for our sakes.

We pray in Christ's name. Amen.

Nature

In all ways, we are conscious of your presence, ever-present God. We look inward, look outward. We reach out, we draw in. We give, we take. And you are there.

We are conscious of you, creator God, through the joy of living, through our environment with its awe-inspiring landscapes, even out to the larger cosmos. Our wonder grows as we relate it all to you.

Most of all, we know you through the glorious life and unmatched sacrifice of your son Jesus, our Christ. For these sacramental reminders of bread and wine, we give you thanks in Jesus' name. Amen.

Labor Sunday

We praise you, ever-working God, for skills to do our work and opportunities to serve. In the midst of this eucharist, we remember and give thanks for the work of Christ and its impact on our lives.

As we break this bread and share this sacrificial token of your struggle to make goodness and love prevail for everyone, may we be worthy to share in your service to humanity. Encourage us when dispirited. Restore our trust when doubtful. We look to you for hope. We choose to live fully and faithfully in you.

Continue to enlighten us about how fully you trust us as your laborers in the field of life.Remembering again the sacrifice of your son, we pray in his name. Amen.

Reconciliation

Wise and wonderful God, work in and through us as we come together around this table of communion. We rejoice in the friendship and love that brings us together. Expand our wonder at the power of this celebration to unite us. Let it free us from old hates and hurts as well as reconcile us to you, to our inner selves, and to our enemies. We give thanks for this bread (*and/or cup*) and for all it (*or they*) represent(s) as we pray in the name of Jesus Christ our Savior. Amen.

Reconciliation and Renewal

O God, as we take the cup of blessing in our hands, we accept it as a gift to ourselves. As we put the cup of remembrance to our lips, we recognize it is filled with the wine of sacrifice and salvation.

As we drink from the cup of reconciliation, we know that we will be changed and renewed. We give thanks for our Lord Jesus Christ from whose hands we received this cup and in whose name we pray. Amen.

World Communion

God, we worship you among our familiar surroundings, finding again your love and compassion that brought your son to the cross. Today we share the strength of others worldwide who in this sacramental manner pledge their lives to your Church.

When we take again this "bread for the world" and this "cup of salvation," we know they are neither toast nor token.They represent not a slight injury but a body broken, not a drop or drops but a pouring out of life, a bloodletting. May we be made worthy, while knowing how unworthy we are. May we be grateful, ungrateful as we can be. May we be trustworthy, fickle as we have been. In Jesus' name we pray. Amen.

World Communion

We come, alone or with family.

We come, first-time visitors or longtime members.

We come, symbolically linking hands with Christians
across continent and island.

We come, deepening our knowledge of traditions
similar to our own and seeking to understand and
appreciate those different and dissimilar.

We represent different languages, and our worship is
casual or formal.

We meet in city squares, or in secret venues; in
cathedrals or grottos.

God of the countless millions, unite us that our
thanksgiving may reach you from every part of the
earth.

Now we ask you to bless the bread and wine, the
representations of Jesus' body and blood.
Strengthen us to praise you with joy for our whole
life.

Amen.

Ministry

Your son's servant ministry showed us, O God, the way of love and sacrifice. In accepting this bread (*and/or wine*) of the sacrament, we pledge ourselves to live for you and to serve you.

As Jesus gathered his disciples around him in the upper room, so we come this morning awaiting your word of peace, asking your forgiveness, and thanking you for your loving sacrifice.

We remain on high alert to the pain and suffering in today's world. We know only time separates us from the first day you shared this feast with the Twelve. May it be as life-changing for us as it was for them. In the name of Jesus, we pray. Amen.

Autumn

God, our sustainer, we come in this season to celebrate the abundance of your gifts spread before us in field and garden. Especially, we thank you for the harvest from which we see:

Grain ripening that with yeast can become bread;
Grapes ripening that when fermented can become wine.

As these products of workers' hands and your gift of life and growth are now placed before us, we give you thanks. When you bless these as a sacrament, we receive them as tokens of Jesus' body and blood. In his spirit we pray. Amen.

Reformation Sunday

God in whose presence we are humbled, we give thanks for this sacrament that unites us with your people, both in this sanctuary and in churches everywhere. Make us eager participants wherever the church reforms and rejuvenates itself. Accept our gratitude for courageous pioneers whose depth of understanding of your truth keeps the Church vital and true.

In praying over bread to be broken and wine to be poured, we reawaken our allegiance to you through Christ. While asking your blessing on these essentials of the great supper of the ages, we invoke your blessing on each one gathered. In Jesus' name, we make this supplication. Amen.

All Saints' Day

Loving God, we have heard your word and obeyed your summons to gather in worship and sharing. At this holy table, we crowd around to recognize saints who have suffered and set examples. We venerate the lives of those who with supreme patience have witnessed to what they saw as your truth. In gratitude to you, we give special thanks for those who lived as prisoners or died as martyrs.

For their lasting vision, we thank you.

For their tenacity, we give praise.

For their singleness of purpose, we express admiration.

So unite us with our Christian sisters and brothers that we may partake in a worthy manner of this bread (*and/or cup*), this sacrament that tells us again of Christ's love for us. Stir our faith, extend our hope, and vitalize our love. We pray in the name of our friend and savior, Jesus Christ. Amen.

Thanksgiving

We give thanks for all of your goodness to us, O God. As we receive and eat this bread (*and/or drink from this cup*), we are reminded of Christ's sacrifice for us.We know our gratitude is little more than a pale recognition of the greatness of your love and willingness to suffer for us.

We are grateful for the whole world that surrounds us with the bounty of harvests and the beauty of so many things you have created. These visions but remind us and relate us to your giving and your saving truth and action. In Jesus' name. Amen.

Thanksgiving

Ever-giving God, from this small element within this cup, we gather mighty meaning. We pause in our whirl of activity to render thanks for your mercy, your favor, your grace, as held out for us in this eucharist.

On this day, we extend our thanksgiving for this opportunity to worship, for the gifts of family, and for the support and nourishment of our church. As we think of the gratitude of pioneers, we reflect on their faith, tenacity, and dedication.

We confess before you our willingness to clutch the freedoms we have and our hesitation at sharing with others. We admit to complicity in hiding truth when others might gain enlightenment, hiding reality for fear of criticism or retribution or lost favor.

As we open ourselves before you at this table, give us courage and strength through a vision of the sacrifice of your son, our savior, Jesus Christ. Amen.

Thanksgiving

O God, we come to this feast with thanksgiving for the death it portrays and reenacts before us. Even more we thank you for the resurrection life it represents. We go from this communion with thanksgiving for new life revealed in Christ's redeeming love.

Together we accept this emblematic bread as we give thanks at this season for other blessings, small and great. When we join with others who through the years have celebrated this season, we give thanks for bounty beyond our deserving.

Keep us true to our faith. Renew our loyalty to our mission. Unite us in accepting and making real to the whole world this "once for all" sacrifice. In Jesus' name, we pray. Amen.

Thanksgiving

With gratitude we assemble, O generous God. We come with thanks in this season of feasting and celebrating. Be present with us in all of our rejoicing. Be present with us in our moments of remembering your sacrificial love for us.

As we gather around your table, unite us not only in partaking of the sacred elements. Unite us also in the fellowship of saints present and past, of Christians nearby and far away; of people bound together in sacramental ties, one to another and to you. Bless this loaf and cup with your divine approval.

In Christ's name, we pray. Amen.

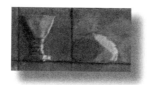

Special Occasions & Subjects

- The following prayers bear subject titles.

- They may be used at any appropriate place in the liturgical calendar.

- They are entered here in alphabetical order by subject.

After Baptism

As witnesses, we continue in this service, giving thanks to you our God for each person who today shared in the dedication of life to Christ through baptism. May this first communion stand for them as part of a life-changing, life-enriching experience, filled with a sense of the holy.

As Christians, we surround this table confessing our need for your acceptance and forgiveness as we acknowledge our weaknesses and transgressions. Measure our lives with your grace and generosity.

Unite us in sharing baptism and communion—expressions of Christ's death and resurrection—because they bind us to you and to Christians everywhere. In the embrace of Christ's love, we pray. Amen.

After Communion

We surrendered ourselves to you O God, in this act of worship.We ask you to demonstrate yourself to us afresh. Motivate in us the desire to love you more passionately, to know you with increased depth and intimacy, and to serve you with complete devotion. Grant the blessing of your unequalled peace. Through Jesus we pray. Amen.

Bread

Our God, give us this day our daily bread. We make this request because we know that you alone have power to give or to withhold the process of nutrition and growth. We make this petition because we know that some of our efforts at helping ourselves and supporting ourselves are so inadequate. We make this request knowing that some others we call brothers and sisters, if they had their rights, would have all the bread that is currently available, today, tomorrow, next week, and for the rest of this decade.

We pray that we may continue to be fed no matter how little we deserve it. We beg you to continue to sustain us in spite of our reluctance to share with others who have never had enough bread and never will.

Although we realize there is audacity in our continuing to petition you for our daily bread, we ask you to do this as a condition of our increased willingness to share what we have. Beyond that, we know we will continue to exist on borrowed bread.

We particularly thank you now for this symbolic bread dedicated as memory and sacrament of Christ. In his name, we pray. Amen.

Bread

Bread, rising with yeast, makes us conscious of your spirit within us, creator God. Fresh bread—baked, enriched—makes us aware of newness and vitality within your Church. A loaf on this table draws us to the special, the sacrificial, and the sacramental as we ask for your blessing.

Grant us the richness of this whole experience as we appreciate not just family, close friends, acquaintances—Christians in this sanctuary—but link us to yourself and Christians everywhere in the bond of this special meal. Keep far from us the flat, half-baked, and the stale. Awaken our memories of the real dimension of this supper we know in the arrest, trial, crucifixion, and death of our Lord. Most of all, allow us to share in Christ's resurrection and eternal presence. Amen.

Candlelight

God of bright stars and suns, God of all strength and mighty power, we come to worship you. At this time, we also revel in the subtleness of flickering candlelight—its gentleness and allure.

We search in this setting for a deeper, different meaning to life and all that it brings us. Open up rays of truth, possibilities only divine power can reveal.

In the broken bread and poured wine, remind us of your redemption made accessible for each one of us. Bless each of these elements to enhance life through the suffering and sacrifice of Christ. In his name, we give you thanks. Amen.

Challenge

As we come to share again in this feast of remembrance, all-knowing God, we relate to Christ's sobering words, "One of you will betray me." Before we either accuse or excuse ourselves, help us focus on your mercy and willingness to forgive.

Unite us around this table as we elevate before you and ask for your blessing on the loaf and cup. Bring your new spirit of holiness to us as we share bread and wine. We see vividly the connection between the Last Supper and Christ's crucifixion.

Continue with us as we aim for lives of fidelity without wavering, faithfulness without reservation. We pledge ourselves to make our Sunday prayers become our Monday deeds of service and giving. In Jesus' name. Amen.

Changed Lives

God, whose risen son we worship and endeavor to
    follow, we give you thanks for transformed lives.
As we surround this holy table, the bread and wine
    that we bless remind us of Christ's sacrifice built
    on his service and devotion to all people.
Elevate for us the spirit of caring, the holiness, and
    the deep meaning of these elements as we now
    partake of them.
In awe, we pray through Jesus our Christ. Amen.

Children

On this day for children, we come to you, our God, for blessing. Put us in touch again with their wide-eyed appreciation, their unquenchable enthusiasm, and their effervescent spirits. Unite us again as we seek your divine approval upon the bread and wine which we receive from you and share with one another.

As on this day we rejoice again in childlike qualities of being teachable, curious, and trusting, make us again unstoppable mimics of the way of Christ. For his love and sacrifice, we thank you without reserve. To his service, we pledge ourselves with determination.

Bless those who brought us together. Keep us in all our vulnerability, united in your love. We pray in the name of Jesus, your child. Amen.

Christian Home

We praise you, Divine Parent, for all of the features of wholesome, happy, and healthy living that we seek for a Christian home. Enrich and encourage parents and children gathered this day to worship you.

We praise you, Eternal Giver of the gifts of patience, forbearance, tolerance, and serenity. Engage us in pursuit of these distinctive, outstanding ways of relating together and to our children.

We praise you, Heavenly Lover of the human race, for sacrifice of your divine, your perfect son. Accept our thanks for the essentials of this communion—the bread and wine. Bless them so that as we take them we may be committed completely to your Church and kingdom. Amen.

Confession

We focus our thoughts while we come together
  around your table, O God.
You have spoken to us through Jesus Christ.
Your love has been fully declared to us in his life.
In anticipation, in gratitude, in obedience, in humility
  we come to you.
Once more, we confess our unworthiness to come
  before you because we have failed one another
  and sinned against one another.
Yet with assurance of your willingness to accept
  us, we come with thanksgiving as we accept
  this bread and cup in symbol and sacrament of
  Christ's death for us.
In his name, we pray. Amen.

Contrition

Before you, O God, we come with open minds,
not because we have forgotten, but because we
remember. We come for spiritual renewal, not
because we have no confidence in ourselves, but
because we have more confidence in you.

We come to extend hands and hearts in welcome
to your children. Here in this sacramental bread and
cup, we take from you what we cannot claim to do or
devise on our own. We need you, gracious God. Bless
us in Jesus' name.Amen.

Covenant

This cup of the new covenant reminds us, renews us, and gives us something eternally new from something old. We thank you, God, for this gift to us. With this sacramental encounter, may we receive new life, may we visualize a new sign of love, and may we give ourselves afresh to your cause.

Help us as we swallow these drops to taste with new understanding and realize a personal renewal at the place of Christ's death. O God of sacrifice, for giving away all that was precious and worthwhile of the life of your son Jesus, we give you thanks. Amen.

Covenant

O God, we rejoice in this concentrated symbol of your love and concern for us. We thank you for this sacramental reminder of Jesus the Christ. Bless us in partaking of this bread that it may be a true celebration of all that is holy between you and your Church.

While we confess again our unworthiness, we hasten to give you thanks. Unite us again to your kingdom of love, relate us again to Christians everywhere. Make us conscious of all generations who have called you Lord and Savior. In Jesus' name. Amen.

Cup

God, when we bring this cup to our lips, we consider the refinement and aging of divine purpose that has taken place. We ponder the purity of the one who made it possible for us to share in the life it symbolizes.

Knowing how weak, or sour, or watered down our lives may become, we taste again the sacrifice that made this perfection possible. It is with wonder that we accept it as a gift we claim, just as we know you invited us to share in it.

Let us savor it, remember it, and relate again in this mystic feast of love to the Savior who invited us to gather as his guests. We come in thanksgiving, just as we come in Christ's name, asking your blessing. Amen.

Cup

Surprise us with your presence, gracious Lord, just as you surprised and disturbed the disciples when they communed in Emmaus. We thank you for this cup and just as enthusiastically thank you for all your goodness, O God. May we visualize you as risen, as vital, as close, and related to us—our spiritual reality and blessing.

As we receive again the fellowship and the renewal, may we prepare spiritually to stand up as Christians both to our inner struggles and temptations and to any challenges directed to our path from the outside world. Teach us again in the receiving of this cup to share one another's burdens and be sensitive to the dangers of betrayal. We pray in the name of the one who shunned no trial, even Jesus Christ. Amen.

Evening

Daylight disappears, and we come to you, ever-living God. Carefully enfold us and secure us in your protection.

Evening suggests thoughts of benediction on the day, so we come to you for blessing.Accept the offering of praise we bring you, as we also bring our confession of flaws and desire for your pardon.

Night wraps around us, and we know your love is surrounding us forever. Bring us around this communion table to feel your closeness in each element of the sacrament. Upon them, we humbly ask your blessing.

Daylight will dawn, and we have confidence in its appearing, as in your ultimate triumph. Speak to us again through the sacrifice of Christ as we see the light of his victory in the resurrection. Amen.

Grief

God of us all:

We come to your table, the satisfied and the needy.

> May those who come with grief gain a glimpse of joy.

> May those who come with anger go with calm.

> May those who come with stress go with peace.

> May those who come with resentment go with delight.

> May those who come with fatigue go with new vitality.

> May those who can, share hope and faith and joy.

We give thanks for this bread (*and/or cup*). Make it (*or them*) rich with your blessing.

We renew our vows to Jesus Christ, whose gift and sacrifice it is.

May we all leave renewed and challenged.

Amen.

Guests

Living God, we come to your table. We would come even for the crumbs beneath it, but we gather as privileged, invited guests.

Loving God, we long for your blessing and your acceptance. We come with assurance that you are forgiving us.

Longing God, we know you wait for our return from the prodigal journeys that we make in our minds and in our actions. We know you are waiting with this feast of welcome.

As we reach out to break this bread (*and/or drink this cup*), this sacrament, this token of Christ's crucifixion, we ask you to bless it. To you, our God, we give thanks, in Christ's name. Amen.

Guests

At your invitation, O God, we come with eagerness and anticipation. How can we be your guests? We know we do not deserve the honor of being at your feast.

When we see what you have prepared for us, we give thanks. We receive this bread and this cup, knowing their life-giving power.

In Jesus' name we commune, remember, and ask forgiveness. Continue to bless us, we pray in Jesus' name. Amen.

Faith

We join you, O God, around this table, in this fellowship, and with all the saints, asking for your forgiveness. Speak through these elements that remind us of and link us to your son's service and sacrifice.

Bless all who have cherished the eucharist, kept the faith, and now trusted it to our care. Prepare us for undertaking more of the mission of the Church to the uninvited, the excluded in our neighborhood and nation, in our city, and around our world. Enrich each person who shares in this feast and shows your love to others. We pray in Christ's name. Amen.

Forgiveness

We give thanks to you, merciful God, for the sustenance, strength, and enrichment received from this communion element—the bread (*or the wine*). Around this holy table we associate as the forgiven—

forgiven before and beyond our need for
acceptance,
forgiven beyond our willingness or ability to
forgive others,
forgiven by your generosity and love.

With joy, we celebrate our new beginnings. We celebrate because of the challenges and commission we have received from our Lord. In these moments of devotion, we renew our allegiance to the one who made this eucharist possible. We reach out in caring for one another in times of happiness as in times of grief and distress, through Jesus Christ our Lord. Amen.

Forgiveness and Renewal

We come, O God, as guests to your house, to your table, to your feast. We come not as customers to bargain, barter, or buy. We come as sinners forgiven, and in our worship we give thanks for this bread (*and/or wine*).

As we accept the gift, symbol, and sacrament, we search for its deeper meaning. In Christ's self-denying surrender of his life—his body and blood—we find love beyond our imagination, greater than any other human gives. Renew us as we pray for forgiveness and ask to share your love.

In Jesus' name, we pray. Amen.

Harvest

Benevolent God, you have provided abundantly for our physical needs, sustaining our bodies Throughout this harvest season, we give thanks for your bounty and for all the ways in which you have been generous with us.

We pray, as we join around this table to receive again the bread (*and/or the wine*) of your love and sacrifice, that here we may receive the harvest of your provision for our spiritual needs. We grapple again with our being undeserving and our turning aside from your generosity.We give you thanks in Jesus' name. Amen.

Homebound

God, we pray for your closeness and blessing upon each person in this dwelling. We celebrate with Christians in every part of the globe as we remember your son in this communion meal.

Surround each of us with your strength, your comfort, and your love. As we focus on the intimate gathering where Jesus and his disciples met in the upper room and broke bread together, may we sense a similar bond.

Bless, for our spiritual nurture, the bread and wine before us. We thank you humbly for Christ's sacrificial giving of his body and blood for our sakes. Continue to guide us each day of our journey through this life. Amen.

Humility

With humility, Jesus in washing his disciples' feet demonstrated for all of us this virtue. God, we pray that our actions may include similar acts of gracious servitude.

Anchor our thoughts in the truth that our Christian commitment is to unite in giving service, not in gaining status. Prepare our minds with this attitude as we commune together today.

Grant the enrichment your blessing brings to the bread and wine—to every thought, every act connected with this sacramental supper. Center our minds on Christ's voluntary surrender of himself for our sakes. Amen.

Humility

Gathering, as we are accustomed, we know we are guests at your table, O Lord. We experience your welcome as host. As we think back on the humility with which you washed your disciples' feet, we wonder whether we would welcome the attention or react with aloofness like Peter.

We thank you for the grace shown when you associated with Simon the leper, a Samaritan woman, and a deranged Gadarene man. Help us to keep our boundaries low and our welcomes wide.

Now we confess our pitiful justification for our own presence here, as we ask your blessing on ourselves and upon the bread and cup representing your sacrifice at Calvary. In humility, we would serve you. Amen.

Infant Dedication

New life stirs feelings of expectation and hope in us, loving God. As we have witnessed the presentation and blessing of these infants and commitment of their parents, we give thanks and praise you for the miracle of life and all the delights and challenges it affords us.

Now, O Divine Parent, as we share with your family in this meal of remembrance, bless, we pray, the elements of which we will soon partake. Keep vivid in our minds the dedication you demonstrated for the complete human family with the sacrifice of your son on our behalf.

Never let us leave this eucharist without sharing the awe of Christ's great love. Be with us in our resolve to join with these parents as they provide nurture and encouragement, both in their days of exultation and in struggles to fill with honor their responsibilities to their children. Amen.

Joy

Today we share the joy of this celebration,
just as at every eucharist we look forward from the
crucifixion to the resurrection, to the victory of Christ.
We praise you, dear God, for the blessing we receive,
the uplift to our spirits, and the exuberance that
surrounds us each time we commune.

Take from us, as we make confession, those
failures and faults that obstruct us, rendering us
pale copies of your son's perfection. Receive these
symbols of your body and blood, blessing this bread
and wine that we are about to receive.

Thanksgiving comes from the depths of our
beings as we relate in this cherished setting with
fellow guests gathered today. We are conscious of
the servants and saints who through the centuries
faithfully brought your truths to us. Amen.

Leaders' Installation

Our communion again brings before us giving, sharing, sacrifice, and responsibility. God, make us aware of the debt we owe to our Lord as we bring this bread and wine for your blessing. When we come before you in this memorial feast, we remember Christ as he requested and give thanks for his offering of himself on our behalf.

Surround each of our chosen and dedicated leaders with your strength. We promise them our support as we work together for the extension of your Church in our community and around the world. Let each task be consecrated, each decision directed to the edification and unity of Christians and the coming in its completeness of your kingdom. Amen.

Light

Creator of light, we come out of the darkness in which we stumble repeatedly. As disciples of old experienced enlightenment when they met their Master around the table, may we also share in the knowledge and understanding the Eucharist brings. As we surrender our lives to you, take from us the confusion, the disarray, and the carelessness that keep us blinded to your revelation.

Forgive us where we need your acceptance. Renew us where we have become lethargic. Accept us where we feel ostracized. We take with gratitude and thanksgiving this bread (*and/or this cup*), receiving it (*or them*) as an undeserved gift. Our prayer is in the name of Jesus Christ, whose life and sacrifice we now remember. Amen.

Music

In your presence, O God, we are awed and silenced. We have marveled at the ecstasy of music both in rousing, crashing beats and in calming, gentle notes.

Make us receptive to the inspiration and skill that brought together the composers' conception and the musicians' presentation of these divine sounds. In the stillness, we pray in thankfulness for the blessing of our Savior, Jesus Christ, whose life and death bring us to you.

We praise you in word and music, reaching out to those around us in tribute for all your gifts, especially in thankfulness for this bread and wine. Bring us harmony when we contemplate their sacramental meaning. We accept both our proneness to error and your powerfulness to save. In Christ's name, we pray. Amen.

New Members

God, surround us all with your love. Encircle our new Christians as you have embraced the rest of us through the years.

God, fill us all with your peace. We ask you to surround our new Christians as you have fenced us in with your security.

God, pervade us with your hope. We ask you to spread through our new Christians with holy anticipation as you have encompassed us through the years.

Now, as we bow in your presence at this communion table, we show appreciation to you for this bread and wine. Bless them to each of us as we remember the one who gave himself for us. May his cruel, inexcusable death speak to us of the ultimate sacrifice. In Jesus' name, we offer our entreaty. Amen.

Ordination

We pledge ourselves to serve you, O God, as we grasp
the magnificence of your call. In the company of
countless devoted servants, we stand in humility.
Accept our willingness to serve you now and
throughout our lives.
May we rise to challenges, whether near or far.
May we measure up to the tasks, whether short or
long.
Now, we vow allegiance to your Church, strengthen
us as we accept this bread and wine, signifying
for the generations of your servants the
unconditional surrender of Jesus our Lord. Bless
these elements, and bless us that your spirit may
prevail within our entire ministry, we pray. Amen.

Outreach

God of all people from pole to pole and around the earth, we come to ask for your blessing. As guests, we gather at this table with people who gathered and are gathering in places around the globe. Keep us aware of the great crowd with whom we worship and whose concern for the Church unites and strengthens every one of its members.

In these moments, we make confession of our need for wider-ranging vision. Keep us true to Christ's call to go to the entire world.

While focusing on the prepared bread and wine, we give thanks for them, receive them, and meditate on the broadness, the inclusiveness, and the all-encompassing design you prepared for us. May Christ's sacrifice on the cross bring before us your ever-available benevolence. Amen.

Outreach

When need is presented to us or when opportunities are revealed to us, we sometimes require your nudging to send us into action. Caring God, with thanks we accept your prompting and the strength of your presence to vitalize our witness.

Overwhelming as the needs for food, clothing, and shelter may be, we place them in the perspective of spiritual needs. Aid us as we continue to share material commodities, and, even more, stand beside us as we share gifts of acceptance, support, friendship, and love.

May this bread and wine seal the covenant between us. Bless them and enrich us, we fervently pray in Jesus' name. Amen.

Reflection

God most high, in these moments we pause to reflect on what we are doing here, what is happening to us and to all others gathered with us.

In recollection, we think of Jesus with his twelve
disciples in the upper room.

In awe, we feel the closeness of your spirit.

In dedication, we reaffirm our loyalty to you. Bless the bread and wine we brought and multiply in them the greatness of your grace. As we accept them and pass them over our lips, we recall again our Lord's reference to his body and blood as he instituted holy communion at the Last Supper. Amen.

Retreat

Just as Jesus drew apart with his disciples for his last supper, may we sense your spirit throughout the select gathering in which we share today. God, make us worthy.

Since those of old came to communion with mixed feelings, mixed motives, and mixed resolves, may we be alerted to come with honesty and insight. God, make us a credit to your Church.

As we share the bread and wine, we pray for your divine blessing on them. Bring to us satisfaction that our spiritual needs are met on this unique occasion and with these sanctified elements. In Jesus' name, we offer this thanksgiving. Amen.

Senses

...od, for using our essential
...uth to us through the broken
... Keep us, because of our
...m debasing them to the role

... own up to being less
... intended, to becoming less
... an we promised to remain. Hear our
... on, and grant, if it is your will, a pardon.
... as we taste bread and wine, remind us of their
sacrificial meaning and of their divine nature. Let
us focus on the richness of all your gifts. Make us
willing and eager to continue sharing this feast and
extending it to more and more of your people. In
the name of the Savior, Jesus Christ who sacrificed
himself for our sakes, we pray. Amen.

Service

At this table, O God, where your bounty meets
our need, we gather in wonder. We thank you for this
cup with its drops of sacrificial liquid, a reminder,
sacrament, symbol, and seal of your love and caring.

May your generosity prompt us to added
generosity, your sacrifice trigger our willing sacrifice,
your understanding draw out our understanding, and
your unqualified acceptance inspire our unreserved
acceptance. Help us to apply ourselves in serving
not just the lovable and friendly, but also the critical,
the cranky, the unforgiving, and the unrepentant. In
Christ's name. Amen.

Sharing

God, our redeemer, we give thanks for the bread, prepared again and given again, so that we receive it fresh from you.

We pray for understanding of the thoughts that motivated our Lord as he instituted this sacrament and faced crucifixion. We share in the feelings of love that enticed him to do this on our behalf.

Let our communion be personal and special, and may our continuation as followers of Christ be constant, convincing, and enthusiastic. Bless all who share in this feast today—not only those who are here with us but all others in sanctuaries all around the world. In Christ's name, we pray. Amen.

Shut In

As disciples gathered with the Lord in the upper room, we come as his guests. We pledge ourselves anew to him as we receive the bread and wine in token of his body and blood. We give thanks for his illuminating heavenly truth and for sacrificing his life for us.May these emblems remind us of our share in the whole church and of our continuing fellowship with members of our congregation.

Bless us with spiritual renewal. In Jesus' name, we pray. Amen.

Shut In

Hear our prayers, sustaining God, for those who share today in this celebration of holy communion. We bring memories and prayers of the whole congregation worshiping through the years as they convey to mind the supper Jesus and his disciples shared.

Bless all who are in special need as we dedicate the bread and wine. We give thanks for the witness of those about to share in this celebration.

Relate us back to the gift Jesus wanted to share with us and to his request that we do this "in remembrance" of him. Give us your calm, your grace, your strength as we accept your salvation. Amen.

Stewardship

Whenever we come to this communion table, your gifts and sharing with us, generous God, make all our stewardship look insignificant. We pray for release from being paralyzed and rendered inactive as we pale in your presence.

Wherever we encounter your generous provisions for our life, health, and comfort, we marvel at everything you have done. We pray for sensitivity to all created life, all beautiful and exciting creations.

Whatever we bring as gifts to present to you, whatever pledges and promises we make, we deliver them in faith that you will bless them. As we offer this loaf and cup for blessing, we thank you for the triumph and hope shared with us from your son's death. We pray in Jesus' name. Amen.

Struggle

Merciful God, meet with us today as you have met with your disciples, followers, and saints through the long centuries. Mix again your holiness with our humanity, your spirit with our senses, and remind us of our place in your world and your presence in our lives.

We take the sacramental bread (*and/or cup*) with humility. We sense again the struggle it requires for us to rise above our willingness to drift rather than be directed, to be content with our old biases and hates. Prepare us to bear others' burdens and forgive others' faults. In Jesus' name, we pray. Amen.

Wedding

In these moments of high expectation, we dedicate ourselves anew to you, our God. As your love overlays our love for each other, may we find greater depth and meaning in our relationship as we unite in this celebration of the eucharist.

We thank you for challenging us to new heights of sacrifice and devotion and find in Jesus Christ our Lord the essence of self-giving, unconditional love.

Bless these elements of the sacred rite as we receive them today. Our vows we seal with this bread and wine, as we pray in the name of Jesus.Amen.

Youth

We rejoice, O Lord, in the days of youth with freshness and spontaneity, anticipating goals and achievements, crowded with expectations and hopes.

In this day of celebration, refresh us all as we come to this feast commemorating belief in the resurrection with the abundance of new life that it promises. Bring us your spiritual vitality as we unite in this sacred observance.

Bless, we pray, each essence of the eucharist, the bread being broken and the wine being poured. As we participate, please, God, accept us as we are, knowing what with your strength we can become. In Jesus Christ our redeemer, we entreat you. Amen.

Index